VIGELAND
PARK

VIGELAND PARK

Vigeland Sculpture Park and Frogner Park form Oslo's largest and most attractive urban park. Together they represent an important leisure facility for local folk while simultaneously attracting tourists from all over the word. Nearly two million people visit the park each year.

There are three main reasons why Vigeland Park has a special place in Norway's artistic history and in the hearts of the Norwegian people. Firstly, there is the unique interplay between park landscape and sculptures. One's perception of the bronze, granite and wrought-iron sculptures varies with the season and time of day. Changing light and opalescence in the sun, rain, frost and snow always seem to provide a new experience. The second reason is that Vigeland's art is about life. In his work we see people in all stages of life and states of emotion. We see ourselves in the sculptures and we can read into them our own adventures and experiences in life. At the same time they have a symbolic content that elevates them to universal timelessness. The third reason is that the two hundred or so sculptures were designed single-handed by Gustav Vigeland. This display of artistic strength is not only unique in Norway but also in an international context. Furthermore, Vigeland is also responsible for the layout of the sculptures, the architectural elements, and the design of the park west of the Frogner dams, with its lawns and avenues. There are no other examples in modern times of a sculptor being granted such latitude to exercise his artistic imagination and creative power.

But Vigeland's visions would never have been realised without support from the Oslo municipality and a number of eminent figures from the Norwegian art world. Gradually, donations started coming in from firms and private citizens. The city was eager to accommodate Vigeland and it's people displayed an interest in *the artist* unparalleled in the history of art. It must be remembered that Oslo was a fairly provincial capital at the turn of the century, yet Vigeland was given free rein to erect a sculpture park, according to his own plan and design, despite the immense costs that the city had to bear over many years. To implement such an adventurous project was a giant drain on resources.

The artist signed a unique mutually beneficial contract with the city council. He presented his entire artistic production to Oslo in return for a studio which, following his death, would be made into a museum. Apart from the fountain, Vigeland received neither salary nor commission for the sculptures. Vigeland's plans also presupposed a huge effort from a number of talented craftsmen such as stone masons, gypsum and bronze moulders and blacksmiths. One of the masons' more humble tasks was to transfer Vigeland's plaster models into granite, while the blacksmiths transformed his drawings into wrought-iron.

Surprisingly, the park is not the result of a single overall plan, design or vision. Vigeland worked on the project for over 40 years, during which time he developed the project piecemeal. The idea for the fountain was conceived around 1900; later came the stone sculptures including the Monolith Plateau, followed by

the wrought-iron fencing and gates, and finally the bridge and its bronze statues. The project was still not complete when Vigeland died in 1943. Despite this, the park today is experienced as a single entity, not least because of its geometric permanence and developed character. An 850-metre long axis from the main entrance on Kirkeveien in the east to the "Life Cycle" in the west, represents the backbone of the park. Out from this radiate straight tree-lined avenues and a lateral axis connecting the fountain with the large group of bronze sculptures, "The Clan", to the north. Immediately below the bridge to the south is a circular space with 8 bronze sculptures of infants surrounding an unborn child, which breaks up the strong symmetry of the axial construction. The sculptures along the main axis are located in 5 consecutive units.

THE MAIN ENTRANCE

The main entrance to the park is located on Kirkeveien. It comprises 5 enormous gates and 2 smaller gates for pedestrian access. The first gate designs are from 1926; the

upper elements including the lights were added later. The recurring theme in this distinctive wrought-iron work is the various stylised botanical decorations, dragons, and other fantasy animals placed in circles broken by diagonals and other geometric forms. The craftsmanship and artistic imagery of the lizard-like creatures in the centre gate are particularly interesting; they give the impression of fighting to break free from their wrought-iron shackles. Here we see a recurring theme in Vigeland's work; dragons fighting dragons or dragons fighting people - a fantastical theme with roots in Norse mythology. The dragon may represent the dangerous and evil powers in existence, which gods and mortals alike must avoid at all cost.

Vigeland has presumably been inspired by the dragon decorations on ships and churches from the Viking period and Medieval times. Dragons and reptiles are also depicted in the decorations on the doors of the two gate houses. These simple small bronze reliefs from 1942 are some of the last works made by Vigeland before his death. Perhaps it is no coincidence that they contain seemingly depressing and pessimistic undertones. Creatures attack humans or wind their scaly tails around them. The humans submit and no longer put up a fight. The creatures may symbolise time and the life cycle that keeps people in its unrelenting grip. Just inside the main entrance to the right is a statue of Vigeland by the sculptor himself. He stands in

a smock; hammer and chisel in his hands. His face radiates defiance and aggression - characteristics that must have been necessary to realise the ever-expanding sculpture park. Scepticism to his project grew steadily, not least from his contemporaries who were overshadowed by his genius. But among politicians and the community at large he found broad support throughout his life.

THE BRIDGE

From the main entrance two parallel avenues lead to the bridge. Vigeland replaced the original bridge located here with a magnificent form constructed in granite. In order to accommodate the 58 bronze figures, the bridge had to be built much larger in comparison

to the river it crossed. The sculptures, which were modelled between 1926 and 1933, stand along the granite parapets. Here, as elsewhere in Vigeland's art, realistic portrayals of people are interwoven with symbolic poses. Parents and children in harmonic balance are juxtaposed with themes of eroticism and conflict between man and woman. And the man-to-man relationship and father/child relationship became an interesting and new topic in Norwegian sculptural history. All the figures face inwards or display themselves parallel to the bridge. The line is steady and simple, the designs broad and comprehensive. The most famous of Vigeland's works, the so-called "Sinnetaggen", an angry small boy, is also located here.

Although it does not belong among Vigeland's best sculptures, it has nevertheless become a symbol of the park and Oslo. When it was stolen a few years ago, Norway was almost in national mourning. Never before has a stolen sculpture attracted so much media attention. On either side of the bridge in the middle are symbolic rings; in one float a man and a woman. The ring could symbolise eternity and the attraction between the sexes. Opposite, a man appears to be struggling to break out of his ring - perhaps a representation of time and destiny.

However, Vigeland has not left any thoughts about the symbolism in his work. It is up to the individual to interpret the pieces. There is undoubtedly a religious and mythological element in many of his compositions. This is also evident in the four figural compositions on the high granite columns positioned at the four corners of the bridge. Here, people fight against huge mythical dragons; the most striking of these is a woman who has submitted to the beast in a tender embrace. In many cultures, the dragon is linked to sexuality and fertility.

THE FOUNTAIN

From the bridge the path continues west through a rose-garden to a huge bronze fountain: the oldest part of the park. It is perhaps Vigeland's most impressive sculptural effort - a whole world in relief. In the centre stand 6 giants supporting a huge basin of water - Vigeland has identified one of the giants as himself. The figures represent different ages in a lifetime, and the strength of the individuals vary accordingly. The presentation may be regarded as an act of creation - the great common effort to

give life meaning. The water represents the creative primitive forces that are tamed and held in check by the cultural energy of mankind. The figures were modelled in 1909, with some changes carried out later. Around the edge of the fountain pool are located 20 groups of people and trees modelled between 1906 and 1914. The bronze trees echo the trees in the park. Beneath the crown of the trees unfolds life itself - spanning from birth to death - with all its many facets. Here, for the first time, Vigeland shapes his life cycle theme, where both the sculptures and the reliefs follow in chronological order; from the first child that collects the skeletal remains of its forebears through youth, maturity, old age and finally to death. The last sculpture depicts a skeleton in a tree and reminds us of life's transience. In the accompanying reliefs below, the aged stoop and collapse and transform into skeletons. In mythology and religion the tree is a symbol of life and nature. The same symbolism is found in the trees around the fountain. But many of the works can easily be read as presentations of people in real-life situations: play and establishing a first friendship, first love, birth, family happiness, encounters between grandparents and grandchildren, death that divides lovers. The design of the trees reflect the contour of the centre element of the fountain - the crown corresponds to the basin, the branches and trunk the men. The groups of people are collected in units corresponding to stages in life: childhood, youth, maturity, and old-age. In one of the trees a young boy sits gazing dreamlike over the surrounding landscape - according to Vigeland this is a self-portrait. The idea of the stages of life

and life's cycle is repeated in the 60 bronze reliefs around the fountain edge - modelled between 1906 and 1936. Vigeland has introduced a new theme here: man's relationship with animals. Children play with them, and women show devotion, while the men exhibit a more aggressive relationship. The images are simple with few background details. Vigeland once again shows great psychological insight in the way he portrays human emotions via body language and gesture - arms and hand movements are particularly expressive. Even though many of the scenes in the tree groups and reliefs are products of the artist's imagination and symbolic sense, they have an honest and realistic nature which invites us to interpret them further.

THE LABYRINTH

The area around the fountain is paved in a black and white granite mosaic. The pattern forms a labyrinth which "if solved" is about 3,000 m long. By following the labyrinth from beginning to end you are given a meaningful supplement to the value of the fountain as a whole: it can be regarded as a journey through life with all its dead ends and twists and turns.

THE MONOLITH PLATEAU

After climbing three terraces you reach the summit of the sculpture park; the Monolith Plateau with circular steps and wrought-iron figural gates. From this artificially created plateau you get a fantastic view of the park and its surroundings. Access to this oval, paved area is via eight elegantly designed figural gates in wrought-iron; some of the most original and creative of all Vigeland's works. Here, as elsewhere in the park, the artist depicts people in various situations and in various stages of life. Vigeland allows the thin bar iron to follow the contours of the human form. We can see muscles, ribs, hair and skin folds almost draw in the air by the curved iron bars. In a strange way he gets us to experience perspective and depth in the human forms as they "walk" towards us.

In the centre of the plateau, Vigeland has positioned a 17-metre high column of people called the "Monolith", carved out of one piece of stone (mono = one, lithos = stone). The first sketches of this piece go back to 1919, but it did not find its present form of 121 human figures at three times normal scale until several years later. This is without a doubt Vigeland's most remarkable composition. He never explained it himself, but merely referred to it as his "religion" and insisted that the theme belonged in a world of fantasy. At the bottom of the column lie seemingly lifeless figures. Above them rise a stream of figures in a spiral motion, which appears to slow down halfway before soaring to the top with renewed energy. The column has been interpreted in many ways. Some describe it as a resurrection and fertility symbol, others see it as symbolising the struggle between good and evil. It can also be regarded as a kind of summary of the whole concept of the park: of generations following after each other and building upon each others lives, and the inherent power of life that exists in humankind. The monolith was carved in situ. Three masons worked for 13 years to carve an exact copy of Vigeland's full scale plaster original.

Around the Monolith, Vigeland has positioned 36 granite groups (1915-36) radially down the steps leading up to the monument. As with the fountain, the theme is life´s cycle. Many of the compositions have an ordinary day-to-day character: children playing, adults conversing or helping each other; there are also men in aggressive poses. The simplified and compact figural style ideally suits the hard, coarse grained granite from which they are made. The people appear to be part of the low, square granite plinths. The plinths are so low that only children can stand on them, the adults must kneel or sit. It gives them a heavy and earthbound character.

The path continues towards the west and ends with the "Wheel of Life", a large bronze ring of figures, modelled from 1933 to 1934. The group comprises 4 adult figures and 3 children holding each other to form a closed ring. Once again the circular form is used as a symbol of life's cycle and humankind's passage from birth via death to rebirth. Several larger and smaller sculptures are found outside this main axis such as "the Clan" and "the Triangle".

THE BRIDGE

From the main entrance two parallel avenues lead to the bridge. Vigeland built this magnificent bridge in granite on the site of an old bridge.

Here, as elsewhere in Vigeland's art, realistic portrayals of people are interwoven with symbolic poses. Parents and children in harmonic balance are juxtaposed with themes of eroticism and conflict between man and woman.

24

THE FOUNTAIN

The fountain is perhaps Vigeland's most impressive sculpture - a whole world expressed in reliefs. In the centre stand 6 giant supporting a huge basin of water - Vigeland has identified one of the giants as himself.

The figures represent different ages in a lifetime, and the strength of the individuals vary accordingly.

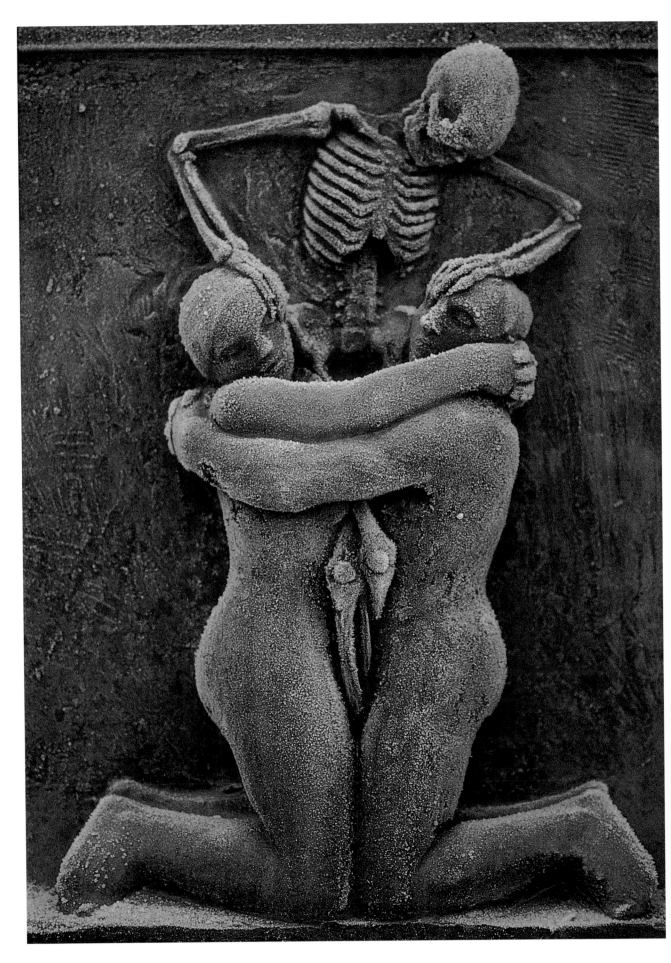

THE MONOLITH PLATEAU

The Monolith Plateau is the highest point in the sculpture park. From this artificially created plateau you get a fantastic view of the park and its surroundings.

In the centre of the plateau, Vigeland has positioned a 17-metre high column of people called the "Monolith", carved out of one piece of stone.

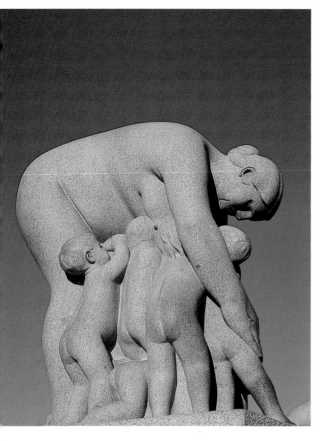

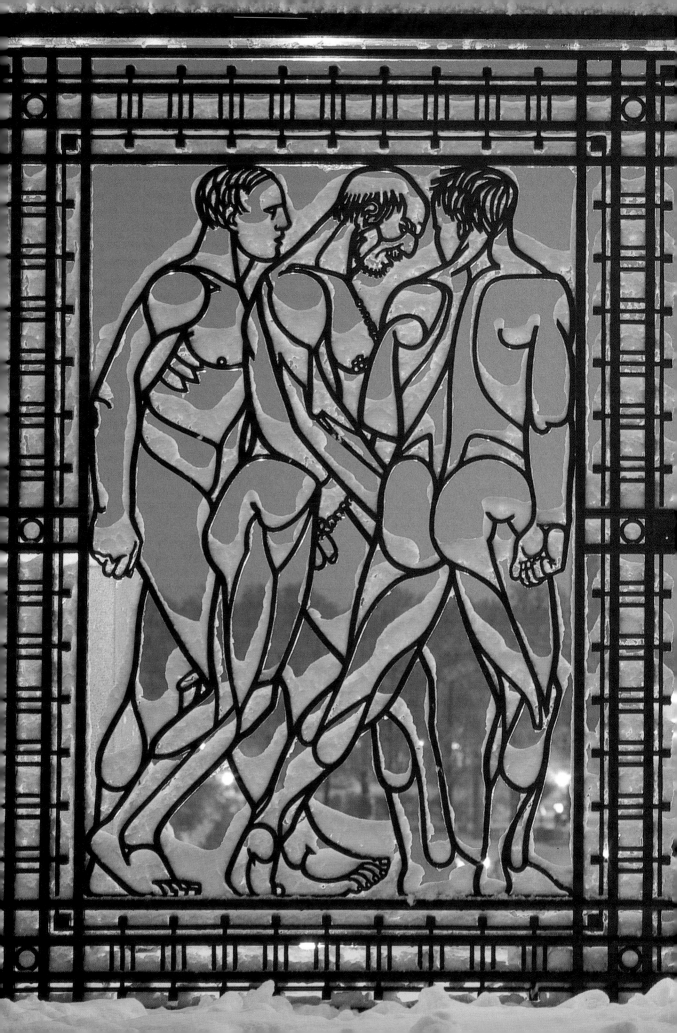

VIGELAND MUSEUM

The museum, just five minutes stroll from the main entrance to the park, houses most of Vigeland's vast production: wood carvings as a boy, romantic images from his youth, his portraits, his designs for statues of famous Norwegians, his drawings and woodcuts and carvings. They show other sides of the artist's rich talent, though all the plaster models of the sculptures in the park are also found here. A number of models, photographs and wall charts relate the fantastic history of the sculpture park and its development through one person's life. The museum, built in the 1920s in neo-classical style, is one of the most beautiful buildings in Oslo. Gustav Vigeland lived and worked here for the last 20 years of his life. Much of the style and atmosphere from that time is preserved in the exhibition rooms. In accordance with his own wishes the urn containing his ashes rests in the museum tower.

56

PUBLISHER:
© Scandinavian Film Group as
Waldemar Thranesgt. 77
N-0175 Oslo

DESIGN:
Skomsøy Grønli as

PRINTING:
Tangen Grafiske senter as

WRITTEN BY:
Fridtjof Bringager
Tone Wikborg

TRANSLATION:
English- John Harley
Japanese- Hiroko Kimura Hjelset
Italiano- Luigi Spada
Deutsch- Peter Marx
Francais- S. Engelshiøen
Espanol- F. Mora
Nederlands- Maaike J. Grit

PHOTO:
Urpo Tarnanen pp 1, 2, 10, 11,
13, 15, 18, 19, 20, 22, 24, 25, 28,
29, 43, 44, 47
Mittet Foto pp 4, 23
Terje Rakke pp 6, 14, 32, 36, 46
Knudesns Fotos. pp 41, 42
F. Widerøe pp 8

Samfoto:
Bård Løken pp 10, 12, 26, 39, 40
Rune Lislerud pp 9
Øystein Søbye pp 13
Trygve Bølstad pp 14, 48
Espen Bratelie pp 18, 37, 38
Kim Hart pp 10, 21, 28, 30, 31,
34, 46
Trym Bergsmo pp 34, 56
Pål Hermansen pp 35
Ole Frøshaug pp 20, 22
Ole Buenget pp 42

Studio Technika:
Atle Karlsen pp 48, 49, 50, 51,
52, 53, 54

COVER PHOTO:
Samfoto
Urpo Tarnanen
Mittet Foto
Terje Rakke
Studio Technika